DECISIONS! DECISIONS!

Thinking and Problem-Solving Activities for PRIMARY Grades

by Imogene Forte
and
Joy MacKenzie

Incentive Publications, Inc.
Nashville, Tennessee

Illustrations by Gayle Seaberg Harvey
Cover by Susan Harrison

ISBN 0-86530-179-4

TABLE OF CONTENTS

PREFACE

Major purposes of the 55 thinking and problem-solving activities in DECISIONS, DECISIONS! are to whet children's imaginations, stimulate higher levels of thinking, and add sparkle and excitement to everyday classroom routines. Additionally, they have been designed to boost vocabulary and reading and writing skills and to afford both individual and group exploration of a variety of problem-solving strategies including: forecasting, decision-making, planning, and productive thinking.

The collection includes: exploratory, hands-on interactive, teacher-directed discussion; research; homework; and long and short-range projects. **All the activities are organized to be easily implemented with a minimum of outside planning and materials organization.** The format and content are complementary to basal and/or individualized programs and lend themselves well to spontaneous use for reinforcement and enrichment of ongoing language programs.

TREASURE TALK

Ask at least four classmates and four adults this question: "If you could keep only two words in the whole English language, which two would you choose?" Write their favorites on the treasure chest below.

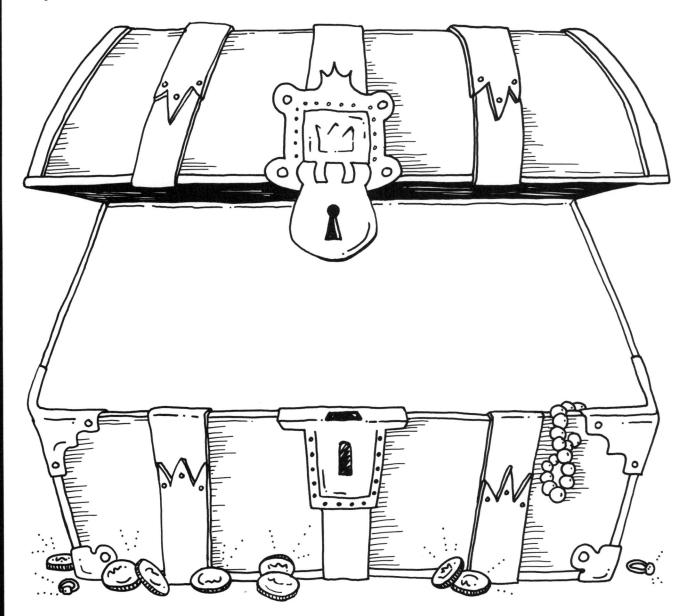

Choose a special part of the school day during which you will listen carefully to your classmates as they talk. Listen for the words you have written on your treasure chest. Each time you hear one of the treasured words used, make a mark beside it. Count to see which words were used most often.

Name _____

Listening, Collecting
© 1991 by Incentive Publications, Inc., Nashville, TN.

LISTEN HERE

PURPOSE

Listening, responding

PREPARATION

Collect "sound making" items. Suggestions:

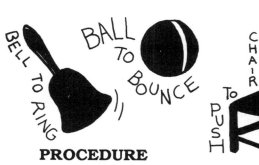
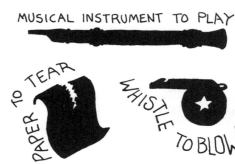

PROCEDURE

1. Blindfold one student at a time and ask him/her to identify the sound being made.

2. Select another student to be the "sound maker." Encourage sound makers to think of different kinds of sounds.

clapping	slamming drawer	laughing
tapping	scraping chalk on board	walking
sneezing	opening/closing door	running

3. When the blindfolded student correctly identifies the sound being made, he/she becomes the sound maker.

VARIATIONS

1. Direct the blindfolded student to identify six classmates by listening to each say, "Listen here."

2. Present students with a tape of sounds (made by the teacher). Students listen to the tape and write answers on paper as the tape is played.

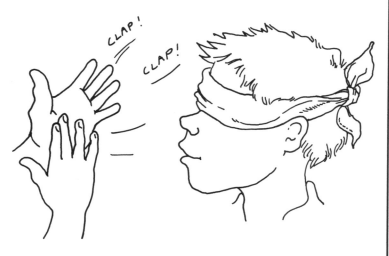

ROUND 'N WIGGLY

Hi! I'm Randy the Round Reptile. I like round things.

See if you can write the name of one thing that is round on each of my sections. Then, color me lightly and cut me out around and around on the heavy black lines. Read your list of round things, and watch me wiggle!

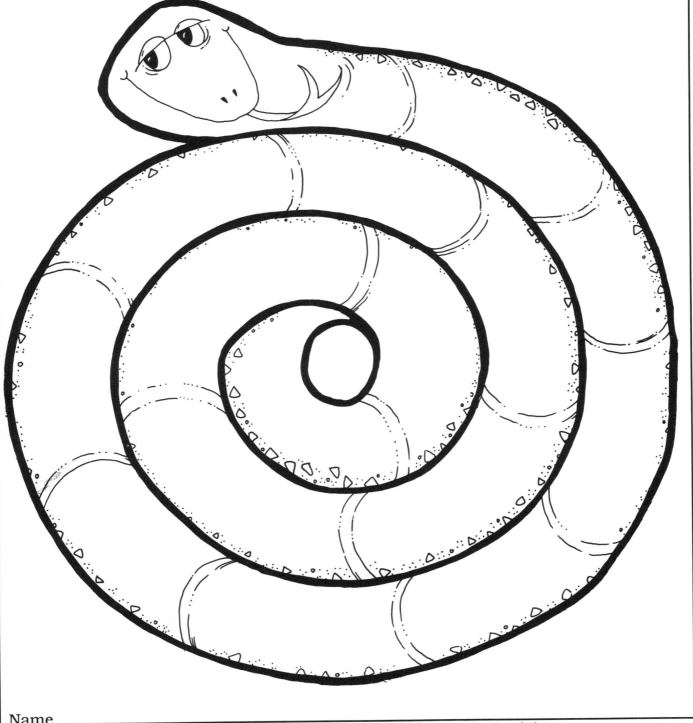

Name _____

Listing, Associating
© 1991 by Incentive Publications, Inc., Nashville, TN.

CATS' NIGHT OUT

You have 5 minutes to study the picture below. Look carefully at each object in the picture. Then turn the picture facedown and put it under your chair. Answer the questions on the CATS' NIGHT OUT activity page.

HAPPY BIRTHDAY ALVIN

Name _____

Observing, Recalling
© 1991 by Incentive Publications, Inc., Nashville, TN.

CATS' NIGHT OUT

Answer these questions without looking back at the picture.

1. How many mice are at the birthday party?

   _____

2. What are they using for a table?

   _____

3. What is the birthday mouse's name?

   _____

4. Is the cake chocolate or vanilla?

   _____

5. How many presents did you see?

   _____

6. Is the tablecloth polka dotted or checked?

   _____

7. Who are the uninvited guests?

   _____

8. Name two ways they are trying to sneak into the party.

   _____

9. Is the weather mostly cloudy or mostly sunny?

   _____

10. How many mice are wearing party hats?

    _____

11. How many cats are in the picture?

    _____

Name _____

Observing, Recalling
© 1991 by Incentive Publications, Inc., Nashville, TN.

KRAZY KALEIDOSCOPE

Cut on the dotted lines and paste the pieces in proper order to solve this picture puzzle.

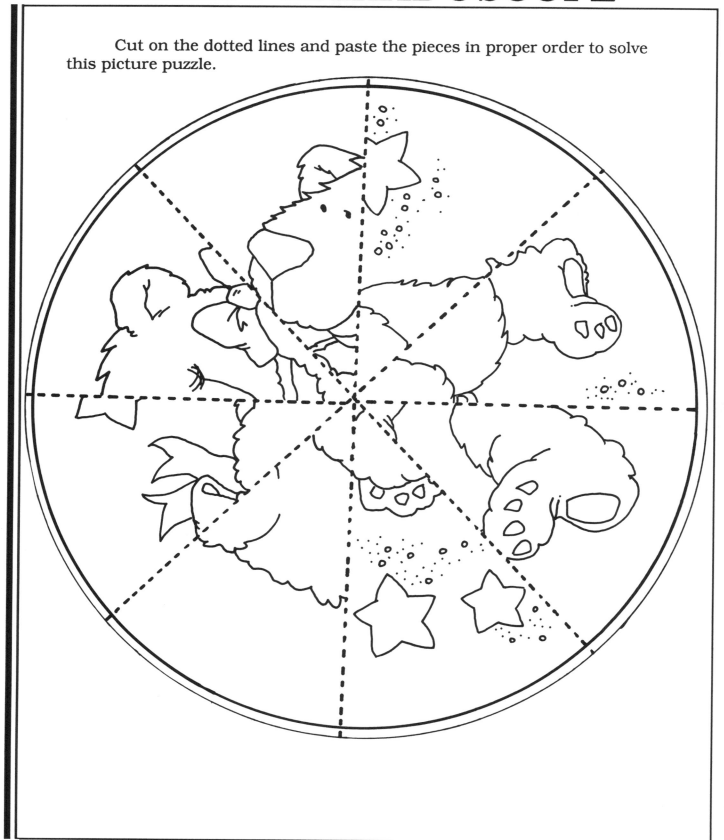

Rearranging, Sequencing
© 1991 by Incentive Publications, Inc., Nashville, TN.

LOST PARTNERS

These partners made a terrible mistake and walked through a mirror. Now they have lost one another.

Hold this page up to a mirror and see if you can get them back together again. Join each pair of items with the corresponding word(s) by drawing a line.

Name _____

Reading, Matching
© 1991 by Incentive Publications, Inc., Nashville, TN.

MOVING DAY FOR MONSTERS

It's moving time, and Mrs. Monster is very busy. Can you help her by labeling some boxes?

Look carefully at the contents of each box. Then cut out the labels on the dotted lines, and paste each one in the correct place.

One label is missing.
Can you write the word for that one?

BONES	TEETH	POTS & PANS
TAILS	TOYS	MASKS
BOOTS	HAIR	

Name _____

Identifying, Labeling
© 1991 by Incentive Publications, Inc., Nashville, TN.

YOU IN A BOX

Take this list home with you. It will remind you of some things that you can collect that will help you tell a story about yourself without any words.

Try to find some of these.

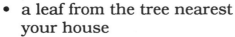

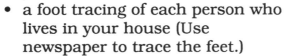

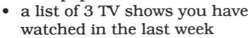

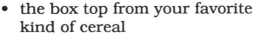

- a picture of you
- a favorite small toy
- a sample of your handwriting
- your favorite T-shirt
- a leaf from the tree nearest your house
- something that is your favorite color
- your favorite book
- a foot tracing of each person who lives in your house (Use newspaper to trace the feet.)
- a list of 3 TV shows you have watched in the last week
- the box top from your favorite kind of cereal
- one small "treasure" that you might keep in your room
- a videotape or CD you enjoy

Bring the things you have collected to school in a box. Arrange the things you have brought neatly on your desk to make a display that tells about you.

Visit the displays of your classmates. Talk about what you have learned about each other.

Name _____

Collecting, Assembling, Organizing, Associating
© 1991 by Incentive Publications, Inc., Nashville, TN.

PEOPLE WATCHING

Looking carefully at something is called observing. Observe each person in your class. Then complete these sentences.

1. A person who sits by me has on the color _____ .

2. A boy who sits near the door has _____ hair.

3. The teacher looks very _____ .

4. The names of two people who have on the same color shoes are

    _____ and _____ .

5. The name of one person who wears

    glasses is _____ .

6. _____ is wearing a shirt with buttons.

7. A girl who has blue eyes is _____ .

8. In this room, there are _____ windows.

9. Someone I like very much has on _____ socks.

10. A boy sitting far away from me is wearing the color _____ .

11. As I was observing, I saw two people smile. Their

    names are _____ and

    _____ .

Name _____

Observing, Relating, Listing
© 1991 by Incentive Publications, Inc., Nashville, TN.

FIVE BY FIVE

Fill in each space with a word that fits the category ABOVE the space and begins with the letter to the LEFT of the space.

	ANIMAL	FOOD	GAME	PLACE	PERSON
F					
B		beans			
T					teacher
S					
P				pool	

Name _____

Brainstorming, Associating
© 1991 by Incentive Publications, Inc., Nashville, TN.

CLOSED FOR INVENTORY

Pretend that you are the owner of a store called "Topsy-Turvy Toyland." It is time for you to inventory – to find out exactly what you have in your store.

Use this inventory sheet to check your stock.

ITEM	AMOUNTS
Number of dark blocks	_____
Number of white blocks	_____
Number of striped blocks	_____
TOTAL BLOCKS	_____
Number of balls with dots	_____
Number of balls with stripes	_____
TOTAL BALLS	_____
Number of small books	_____
Number of tall books	_____
Number of fat books	_____
TOTAL BOOKS	_____
Number of bears	_____
Number of rabbits	_____
Number of ducks	_____
Number of dinosaurs	_____
Number of kangaroos	_____
TOTAL STUFFED ANIMALS	_____

Number of things not mentioned above _____

TOTAL NUMBER OF ALL ITEMS _____

How many more balls are there than blocks? _____
How many more ducks are there than dinosaurs? _____
Of which item is there the greatest number? _____
How many items show an inventory of 3? _____

Name _____

Inventorying, Listing
© 1991 by Incentive Publications, Inc., Nashville, TN.

CLOSED FOR INVENTORY

READY, SET, GO!

In just two minutes, David and Donnie will be late for school! Use your pencil to mark the shortest, most direct route for them to take.

Name _____

Discovering, Conceptualizing
© 1991 by Incentive Publications, Inc., Nashville, TN.

READY, SET, GO!

On this page, make up your own "Ready, Set, Go!" maze. Use a farm scene with two people, four animals, and other ideas of your own. Write your directions in the box at the bottom of the page.

Directions:

Name

Discovering, Conceptualizing
© 1991 by Incentive Publications, Inc., Nashville, TN.

SPORTS MATCH

Draw a line from each pictured object to the name of the sport for which it is used.

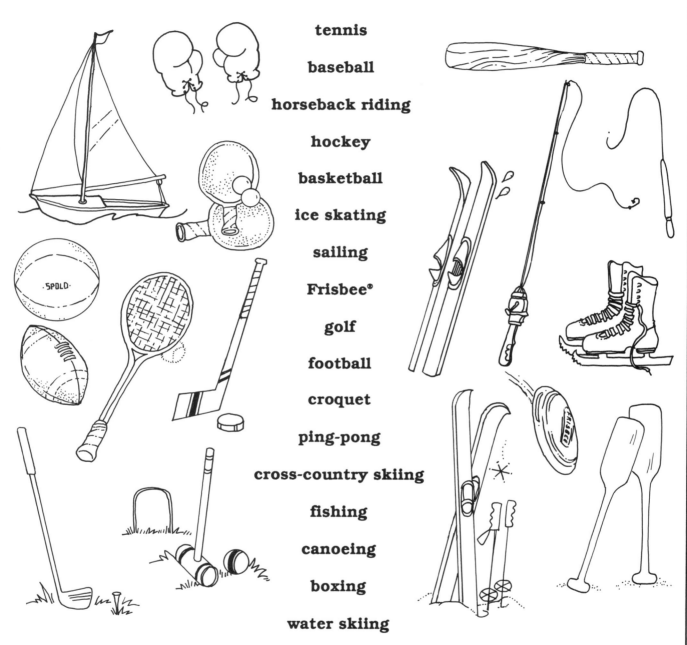

tennis

baseball

horseback riding

hockey

basketball

ice skating

sailing

Frisbee®

golf

football

croquet

ping-pong

cross-country skiing

fishing

canoeing

boxing

water skiing

Put a checkmark by each sport for which a safety helmet should be worn.

Name _____

Matching, Associating
© 1991 by Incentive Publications, Inc., Nashville, TN.

PRIME TIME PLAYERS

PURPOSE

Listening, dramatizing

PREPARATION

1. Practice reading the story "The Bremen Town Musicians" with exaggerated expression, or ask an exceptionally expressive student to prepare the story.

2. Prepare props by coloring and cutting the figures on the pattern pages.

PROCEDURE

1. Choose eight students to play the following parts: a donkey, dog, cat, rooster, three robbers, and a robber spy.

2. Give each character the props provided for his/her part.

3. Read the story aloud as a narration for a pantomime. Direct players to listen for their cues and dramatize the story as it proceeds.

4. After the dramatization has been done several times this way and the characters are familiar with their parts, allow them to say some of their own lines if they wish. (Older students may wish to take turns narrating the story.)

"THE BREMEN TOWN MUSICIANS"

(Adapted from the story by Jakob and Wilhelm Grimm)

Once there was an old donkey whose master was about to turn him out or sell him for glue. Fearful of what might happen to him, he ran away and headed down the road toward a town called Bremen. "There," he thought, "I could surely be the town musician, for I can still bray very well."

He had gone some distance when he came upon an old cat that looked very sad. "My mistress tried to drown me," said the cat, "for she thinks I am too old to do her any good."

"Come along with me to Bremen," said the donkey. "We can make music together." So the two went along until they met an old hound dog whose master had threatened to kill him, and they persuaded him to join their singing group, too.

Later that day, the three came upon a cock sitting on a barnyard gate. The cock looked frightened. "The farmer's wife is going to cook me for Sunday dinner," he crowed. "I must run away!"

"Come with us," chorused the three. So off they all went together to seek a new life and good fortune as the Bremen town musicians.

In the evening, they came upon a house where a light shone in the window. The four companions were very tired and needed a comfortable place to rest. As the donkey was the largest, he went to the window and looked in. "What do you see?" asked the cock.

"I see a table covered with good things to eat and drink and robbers sitting at it, laughing and talking."

"This is the place for us," agreed the four friends, and they began to plan how they would scare the robbers away.

They decided that the donkey would stand with his front feet on the window ledge. The hound would then jump on the donkey's back, the cat would climb up on the dog, and the cock would perch on top of the cat's head. Then they would all perform their music together.

So they took their places. Then the donkey brayed, the hound barked, the cat meowed, and the cock crowed. With that, they burst through the window into the room and scared the robbers so badly that they ran out of the house into the forest.

The four friends sat down at the table and ate as if they would never have a chance to eat again. Then, full and happy, they each found a comfortable place to sleep.

The robbers, who were hiding in the woods, saw the lights go off in the house. Disgusted with themselves for being so easily frightened away, they decided to send a spy back to inspect the house.

The spy crept quietly into the house and went to the kitchen to light a candle. He thought the shining, fiery eyes of the cat on the hearth were live coals, and he held a match to them. But the cat flew at his face, spitting and scratching. The robber spy ran for the door, but the dog, who was sleeping there, bit his leg! As he ran out across the yard, the donkey gave him a kick in the pants. The rooster, watching from the rooftop, crowed loudly.

The robber spy ran back as fast as he could and reported to the leader, "A horrible witch sits in the kitchen and she spat at me and scratched me. By the door is a man with a knife who cut my leg, and out in the yard waits a big monster who beat me with a club. On the roof sits a judge who called out, 'Bring the thief to me!' So I ran away as fast as I could!"

The robbers decided to leave forever, but the four musicians stayed and lived in their house happily ever after.

BREMEN TOWN PATTERNS

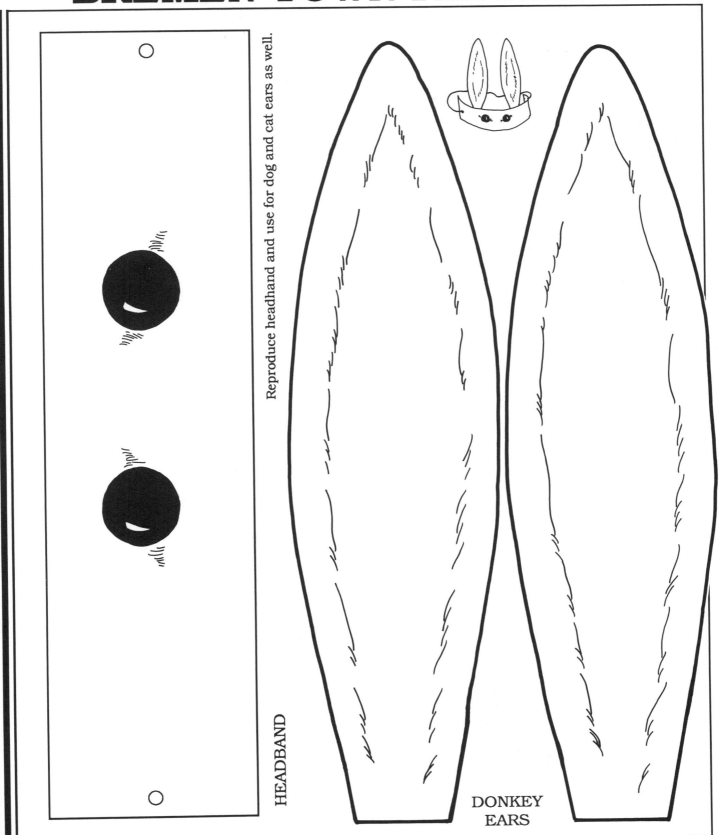

Reproduce headhand and use for dog and cat ears as well.

HEADBAND

DONKEY
EARS

BREMEN TOWN PATTERNS

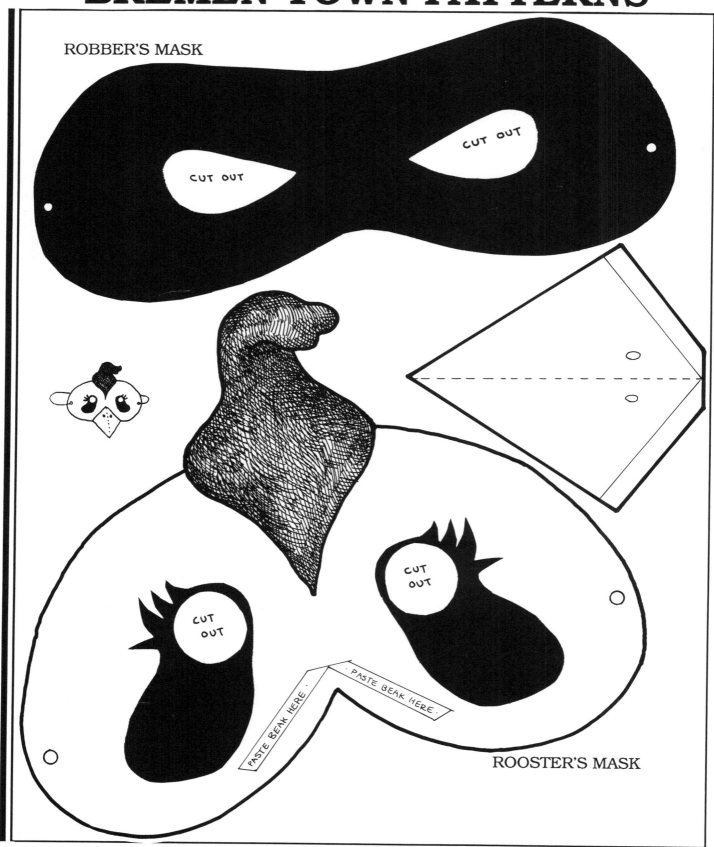

ROBBER'S MASK

CUT OUT

CUT OUT

CUT
OUT

CUT
OUT

PASTE BEAK HERE

PASTE BEAK HERE

ROOSTER'S MASK

BREMEN TOWN PATTERNS

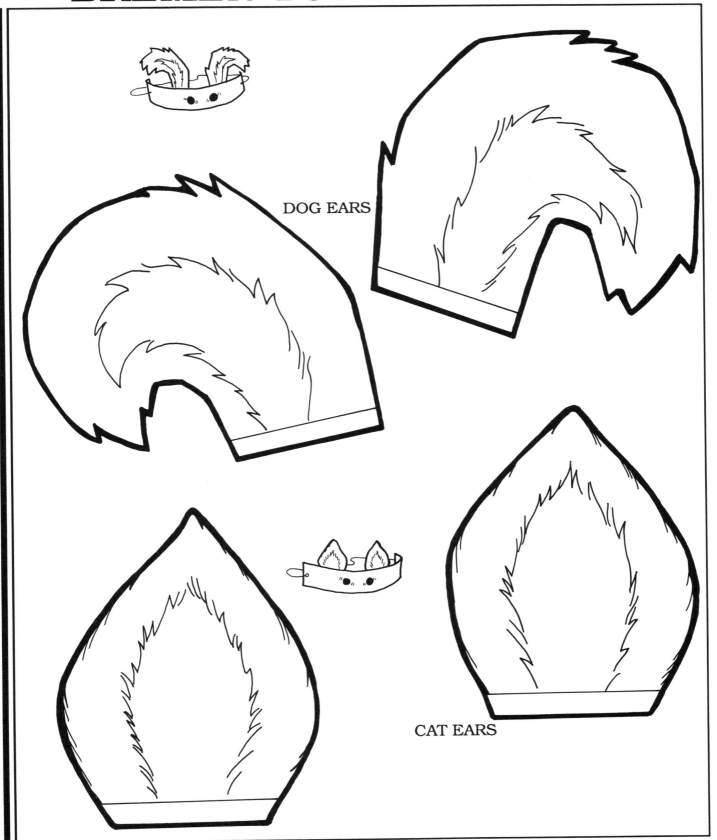

DOG EARS

CAT EARS

PRIVATE EYE I

PURPOSE

Observing, associating, synthesizing

PREPARATION

1. Ask each student to print his/her full name on a strip of paper. Place these strips in a basket or box.

2. Allow each student to draw a name from the basket. If a student draws his/her own name, that strip must be returned and the student must draw again.

3. Provide the following instructions:

PROCEDURE

1. Read the name you have drawn to make certain you know who it is you will observe. (Be careful not to stare...he/she may catch you staring!)

2. Select any day of the week (Monday through Friday) for your observation. Secretly observe and record your person's activities during the selected day. Carefully note times, places, and specific activities like this:

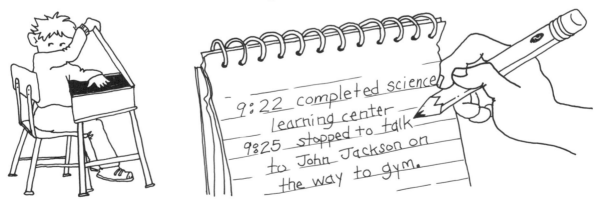

3. Remember, a good private eye needs to be "undercover" and operate in secrecy. The success of your detective work will depend on the person being observed not knowing when he/she is being observed or who the observer is. Keep your written observations private until the teacher gives the class additional instructions.

PRIVATE EYE II

PURPOSE

Identifying

PREPARATION

1. Make an interesting and attractive bulletin board by cutting letters and question marks from colorful construction paper.

2. Arrange the observation note sheets from the PRIVATE EYE activity on the bulletin board. Number them for easy referral.

3. Pin strips of paper or tagboard under each observation sheet so students can write an identity "guess" for each one.

PROCEDURE

1. Ask each student to read at least two observations, guess the identity of the person described, and write the names on the strips under the sheet.

2. Discuss how each guess was made. Encourage students to try to remember traits and habits of various classmates in order to match correct identities with each observation sheet. This will really sharpen thinking skills.

3. It's fun for each student to learn new things about himself/herself from the carefully written, whole-day activity record, as well as see himself/herself through others' eyes as classmates make true and false identifications.

PICTURE POETRY

You can be a poet! Cut the strip of word pictures from the bottom of the page. Complete the poems by pasting each rhyming word picture in its correct place.

If you hear scratching
In my house
Don't worry...It's just
My pet ☐ .

If you want
To clean your room
You will need
A mop or ☐ .

How do you smell
A pretty rose?
You must sniff it
With your ☐ .

When I cannot
Go to sleep,
I count pink ☐
And purple ☐ .

When I can do
Just what I like
I read a book
Or ride my ☐ .

Today, I caught
A giant whale
But I couldn't fit him
In my ☐ . (So I let him go!)

Do NOT sit on
A hill of ants
Or you may have them
In your ☐ .

Name _____

Identifying, Relating, Deciding
© 1991 by Incentive Publications, Inc., Nashville, TN.

WHERE THE TIME GOES...

Keep a record of how you spend your out-of-school time for the next five days. At the end of the five days, you may be surprised to learn just where and how your time was spent.

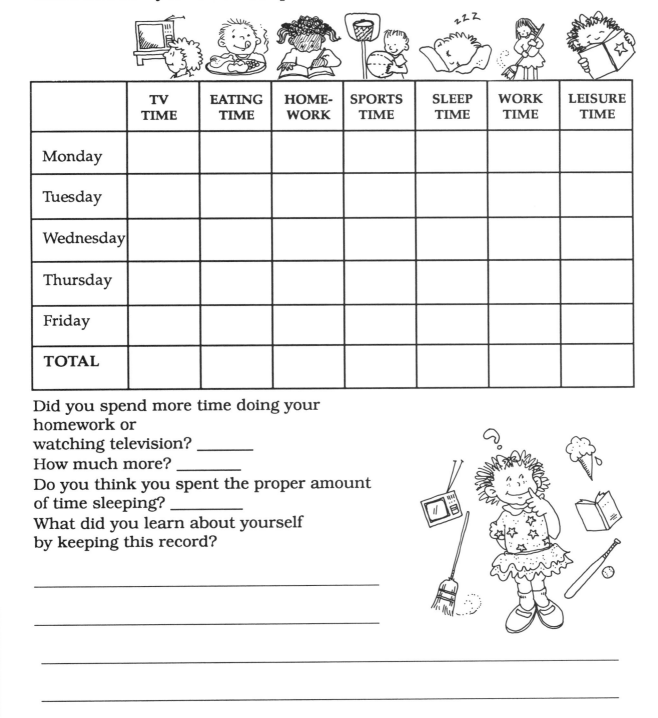

	TV TIME	EATING TIME	HOME-WORK	SPORTS TIME	SLEEP TIME	WORK TIME	LEISURE TIME
Monday							
Tuesday							
Wednesday							
Thursday							
Friday							
TOTAL							

Did you spend more time doing your homework or watching television? _____
How much more? _____
Do you think you spent the proper amount of time sleeping? _____
What did you learn about yourself by keeping this record?

_____

_____

_____

_____

Name _____

Recording, Summarizing, Generalizing, Judging
© 1991 by Incentive Publications, Inc., Nashville, TN.

FEELINGS...

Use just these small spaces to demonstrate four different feelings. Use words or pictures in any way you wish, but make each one unique! (Look up "unique" in the dictionary if you don't know what it means!) You might try an acrostic, haiku, cinquain, simile, drawing, or an idea all your own.

SYMPATHY

LOVE

GREED

FEAR

Name _____

Defining, Interpreting, Minimizing, Translating
© 1991 by Incentive Publications, Inc., Nashville, TN.

GIFTED GIVING

1. Choose a neighbor, teacher, best friend, or a family member for whom you would like to create a special gift.

2. Pretend that you have ONLY the following materials available.

3. Choose any five items on the list to use in creating your gift.

4. Use the space below to draw a picture that shows how your gift might look when it is finished.

- 1 box of whole cloves
- 3 jelly jars
- 1 yard of checked gingham
- a basket of seashells
- 6 spring-type clothespins
- 1 dozen oranges
- 12 yards of polka dot ribbon
- a tin canister of loose tea
- 1 bottle of white glue
- 48 jumbo crayons
- a hammer
- 1 dozen nails in assorted sizes
- a loose-leaf notebook with a pack of lined paper
- a ruler

- 2 small cardboard boxes
- a burlap bag full of peanuts
- six 2" x 4" wooden boards
- a block of paraffin
- 12 sheets of multicolored tissue paper
- 6 pecans
- scissors
- sewing thread
- needles
- 5 chocolate bars
- a handsaw
- 6 safety pins
- 1 package of 4" x 6" index cards
- 1 black, 1 red, 2 green, & 1 blue felt-tip pens

Name _____

Projecting, Selecting, Integrating
© 1991 by Incentive Publications, Inc., Nashville, TN.

LOST!

You are lost in the woods with three friends your own age. You are surrounded by huge trees, and no path leads in or out. The sun has set, and the forest is growing cold and dark. You have only leftovers from your picnic lunch, half a canteen of water, light sweaters, and empty backpacks.

 One of your friends suggests that you should all go in different directions for a short distance looking for a path to follow out of the woods and then return to the spot where you are now and leave the forest together.

The second friend feels very strongly that, since it is nearly dark, the best thing to do is to settle in for the night and wait until morning to try to find the way home.

The third friend has no ideas to offer.

Think about your friends' suggestions. Which do you think is the best idea? Put a checkmark beside that one. In the space below, tell why you chose it.

_____

_____

_____

_____

_____

_____

_____

_____

_____

Name _____

Comparing/Contrasting, Explaining
© 1991 by Incentive Publications, Inc., Nashville, TN.

JUST THREE

Study the pictures. Select the three items you think would be MOST helpful to four people who are lost in the woods. In the big circle, write three sentences to explain why you chose these items and how they would be used.

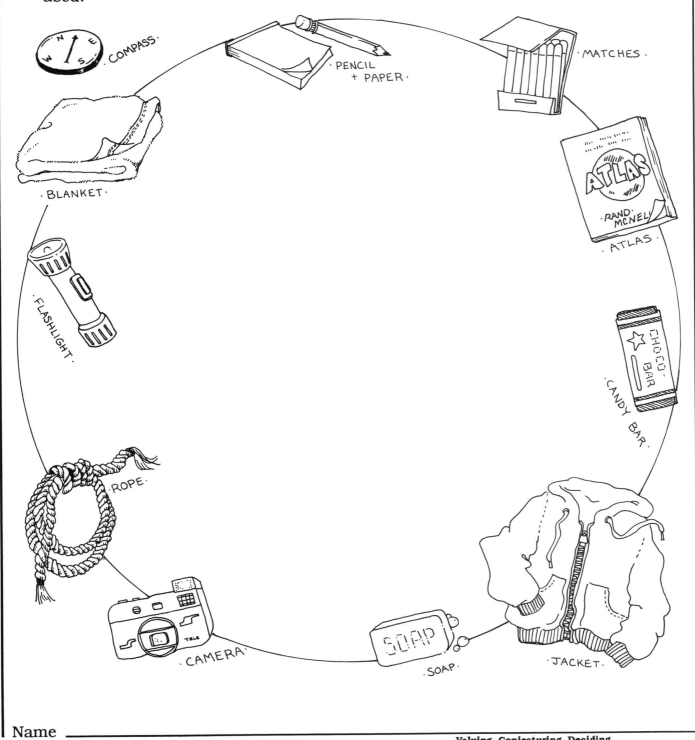

Valuing, Conjecturing, Deciding
© 1991 by Incentive Publications, Inc., Nashville, TN.

GREAT INVENTIONS

PURPOSE

Assembling, valuing, selecting, inventing

PREPARATION

1. Provide a big box of good junk containing these and other materials.

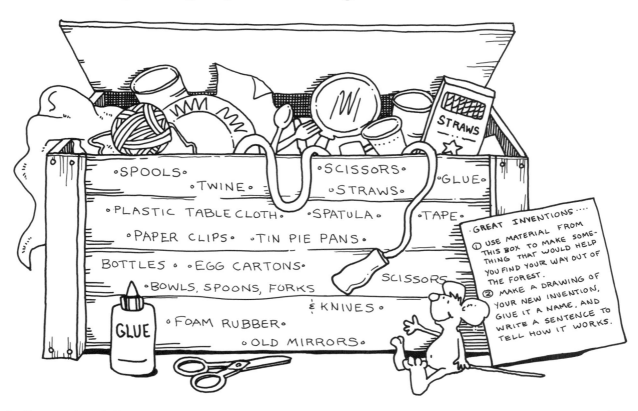

2. Print the following directions listed under "Procedure" on a study guide and place it beside the box.

PROCEDURE

1. Use materials from this box to make something that would help you find your way out of the forest.

2. Make a drawing of your new invention, give it a name, and write a sentence to tell how it works.

ROCK CRITTERS

Make a rock critter as a special gift for someone you like a lot. You will need some small rocks, glue, and acrylic paint.

WHAT TO DO

1. Look for interestingly shaped rocks that will "go together" to make a rock critter.

2. Play around with the rocks until you get an insect or animal that really appeals to you. A ladybug, a fat pig, a turtle, or a bug-eyed creature from another planet might be fun. Don't settle for the first and easiest creation you put together. Experiment with different ways until you have something very original!

3. Glue the rocks together, and let them dry. Then paint on faces or other interesting features.

Name _____

Experimenting, Inventing, Assembling
© 1991 by Incentive Publications, Inc., Nashville, TN.

LET'S HELP PACK!

The Martins are ready to pack the car for their holiday ski trip. Sue and Barbie have offered to put all the extra things in the trunk of the car. Mother has given them three boxes, but they are having a problem packing so many different kinds of things into just three boxes.

While they are working, a friend comes by to visit and suggests that they pack all the things that are alike together and then label the boxes so they will be easier to unpack when they arrive at the ski lodge.

Help the girls get organized by drawing small circles on all the FOOD, small squares on all RECREATION and HOBBY EQUIPMENT, and small triangles on the CLOTHING.

Name _____

Categorizing
© 1991 by Incentive Publications, Inc., Nashville, TN.

LET'S HELP PACK!

Activity Page

Write the name of each item in the correct box. Use your dictionary if you need spelling help.

Name _____

Categorizing
© 1991 by Incentive Publications, Inc., Nashville, TN.

MYSTERY MANSION

Follow these directions to complete this activity.

1. Cut on the heavy black window lines.

2. Fold open on the dotted lines.

3. Paste the front of the MYSTERY MANSION to the matching mansion shape on the mansion activity page.

4. Open the windows and door. Solve the problems you find there.

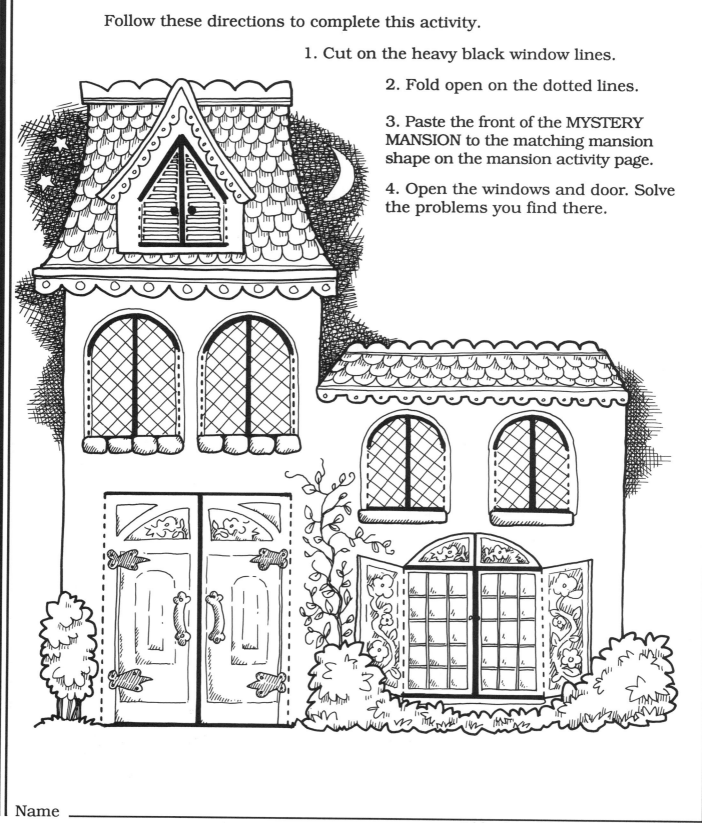

Name _____

MYSTERY MANSION

Activity Page

20 + 7
- 3 + 10 =

John weighs 96 pounds. Mary weighs 54 lbs. How much more does John weigh than Mary?

88
172
244
18
+ 267

739
- 283

4
3
5
9
+ 2

Jim has a marble collection of 312 marbles. He wants to divide them evenly with his 3 friends so that all 4 of them have an equal number of marbles. How many marbles will each have?

Joe has 74 baseball cards. Jill has 55. Bob has 69, and Joy has 70. What is the average number of baseball cards owned by members of this group?

Name _____

WHO'S WHOSE?

Gus and Gabby each have their own private word list. They must choose from the pairs of homonyms in the center list those that match their own. Draw lines to help Gus and Gabby make the matches. (Your dictionary will help you!)

GUS		GABBY
baker	**dough**	deer
	doe	
head	**hare**	rabbit
	hair	
baby	**tears**	cake
	tiers	
muscles	**flex**	spots
	flecks	
pull	**toe**	foot
	tow	
dead	**berry**	fruit
	bury	
boat	**naval**	stomach
	navel	
noise	**creek**	water
	creak	
herb	**thyme**	clock
	time	
smell	**cents**	money
	scents	
weather	**vane**	blood
	vein	

Name _____

Associating, Relating
© 1991 by Incentive Publications, Inc., Nashville, TN.

CREATION SENSATION

Add to each drawing as many lines and shapes as you need to make a picture that goes with the words in that block. It will be fun to share and compare your drawings with your classmates.

Something that grows

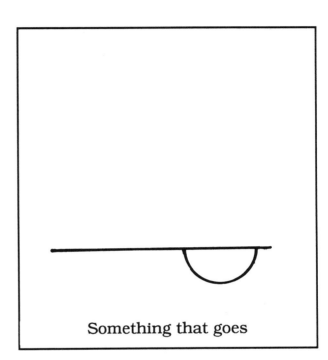

Something that goes

Something for a house

Something silly

Name _____

Relating, Modifying, Creating
© 1991 by Incentive Publications, Inc., Nashville, TN.

A FAMILY PROBLEM

1. Read "A Family Problem" to the group, and lead a discussion of approaches to solving the problem.

2. The most obvious answers will probably be: 1) labeling the food with the name and date, and 2) arranging the food on the shelf in alphabetical order and always putting freshly frozen food on the back shelf so that the previously frozen food will be used first. Guide the discussion to continue until all possible solutions have been presented and cross-examined.

"A Family Problem"

Andrew's mother has a large vegetable garden. She freezes lots and lots of food from it for the family to eat during the winter months. Andrew and his three brothers and four sisters help with the gardening and freezing the foods. They use plastic freezer containers that their mother buys on sale at the corner market, and they save plastic jars to reuse. One big problem they have is knowing what is in what container and which food has been frozen the longest and should be used first.

They freeze string beans, sweet corn, broccoli, red and green peppers, carrots, lima beans, cucumbers, peas, asparagus, and zucchini. Andrew thought of one way to solve this problem, and his sister Amanda thought of another way. Can you think of these two ways and one more?

COMIC CONCLUSIONS

PURPOSE

Sequencing, translating, arranging, abstracting

PREPARATION

1. Cut the same comic strip from the newspaper for two or three days. Be sure to use a strip that builds in sequence from day-to-day.

2. Paste the comic strips in a file folder omitting one or more sections.

PROCEDURE

1. "Retelling a Story" – to show plot and sequence
   • Students write the story told in the comic strips in paragraph fashion underlining the main idea and being sure to include all the details. Remind the students that the pictures help to tell the story, so they must supply words to take the place of the pictures.

2. "Drawing Conclusions"
   • Provide paper and pencils for students to use in drawing the omitted sentences.

3. "Who, When, Where, and What"
   • Students write on their own papers the key words, WHO, WHEN, WHERE, and WHAT. Beside each key word, they write the word(s) from the comic strip or describe the picture from the strip that provides that information in the comic story.

IT'S ALL CLASS!

The objects below can be classified in many different ways. For instance, all round objects could be grouped together, while all objects with straight edges could make up another group. The same objects could be reclassified according to which are usually used outdoors and which are usually used indoors. Other groups could be formed of those that are dark in color and those that are light in color.

Look at all the objects carefully, and complete the lists on the IT'S ALL CLASS! activity page. Then, make as many new classification groups as possible. (Use the back of your page if you need more room.)

Classifying
© 1991 by Incentive Publications, Inc., Nashville, TN.

IT'S ALL CLASS!

Objects with round edges:	Objects with straight edges:

Objects dark in color:	Objects light in color:

Objects found outdoors:	Objects found indoors:

Name _____

Classifying
© 1991 by Incentive Publications, Inc., Nashville, TN.

BUTTONS, BEETS, & BALONEY

PURPOSE

Categorizing

PREPARATION

1. Assemble a collection of many colors of buttons in a sturdy box (a shoe box or a cookie tin will work well).

2. Provide a tray for sorting.

PROCEDURE

1. Direct students to sort buttons using their own system of classification.

2. Ask them to display and explain their system.

3. Allow students who are less able or need more concrete instruction to sort buttons either by color or by size.

ALTERNATE ACTIVITY

Cut pictures of fruits and vegetables from magazines or seed catalogs. Paste them on white index cards and write "fruit" or "vegetable" on the back of each. Print the following directions on the front of a sturdy envelope, and place the cards inside.

"Put the fruits in one stack and the vegetables in another. When you have finished, turn the cards over to check your classification skills."

TO THE RESCUE!

Fill in each blank with the correct word from the list at the bottom of the page to find out what is happening here. Use each word only once.

Caution: There may be more than one way to do it. It takes very careful thought!

"R_____ !" squealed the r_____. "R_____

to my r_____ ! The r_____ old r_____ will r_____

over my r_____ , r_____ r_____ and r_____ them

forever!"

ruin   run   rescue   ride
rabbit   radishes   robot   rush
red   rusty   rosy

Name _____

Inferring, Selecting, Deciding
© 1991 by Incentive Publications, Inc., Nashville, TN.

TO BUILD A BOAT

1. Begin with one letter.

2. Add another letter to that to make a two-letter word.

3. Add a third letter to make a three-letter word.

4. Add a fourth letter to make a four-letter word.

Add letters to build these boats.

Build some more boats that are all your own.

Name _____

LAND OF THE GIANTS

PURPOSE

Imagining

PREPARATION

1. Cut out a pair of huge paper boots for each person in the class. Help students attach these to the front legs of their chairs.

2. Ask each student to bring from home an adult-sized long coat, a pair of old gloves, and a hat.

PROCEDURE

1. Help students stuff gloves and pin them to the coat sleeves.

2. Arrange "booted" chairs in a line or large circle.

3. Make each child a giant by helping him/her don the large coat and hat and stand on the chair with the coat hanging down over the paper boots.

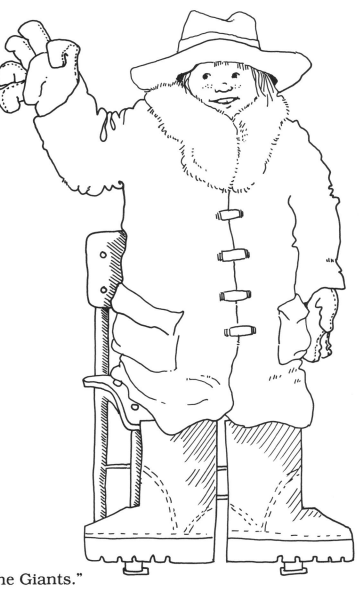

4. Invite a kindergarten or first grade class to visit your "Land of the Giants."

5. Appoint several "giants" to act as interviewers to ask the visitors how it feels to be a very short person in a land of very tall people.

6. When the fun is over, engage students in a language experience in which all contribute to a story about a very small person who visits the "Land of the Giants." The story should focus on how this person feels.

PEEK-A-BOO!

PURPOSE

Hypothesizing, differentiating, brainstorming

PREPARATION

1. Divide students into three groups.

2. Make a copy of PEEK-A-BOO I for each member of group 1, a copy of PEEK-A-BOO II for each member of group 2, and a copy of PEEK-A-BOO III for each member of group 3.

3. Prepare for each student a cover page of dark construction paper in which holes have been randomly punched. Staple one over each activity sheet. Secure at top, bottom, and sides so the student cannot see the activity page except through the holes in the cover sheet.

PROCEDURE

1. Distribute the covered activity pages to the students.

2. Explain to the students that an object is pictured on the covered page. Their task is to hypothesize as to what that object might be by looking through the punched holes.

3. Direct students to consider each hole separately, look at each carefully, decide what the object might be if it appears as it looks through that single opening, and write down that decision beside the hole.

4. After students have considered each hole and made their guesses, they review these and make a general hypothesis of what the entire picture is.

5. Students meet with their groups to share their hypotheses and combine their ideas to make one hypothesis. When this has been agreed upon, students may tear off the cover sheets to check their hypotheses (and color their pictures if desired).

Note: These activity pages may be used as motivation for brainstorming, vocabulary extension, and/or springboards to creative writing.

PEEK-A-BOO! I

PEEK-A-BOO! II

Hypothesizing, Differentiating, Brainstorming
© 1991 by Incentive Publications, Inc., Nashville, TN.

PEEK-A-BOO! III

Hypothesizing, Differentiating, Brainstorming
© 1991 by Incentive Publications, Inc., Nashville, TN.

SENTENCE SENSE

Rearrange the words in these sentences to make two new sentences. Remember, a sentence always expresses a complete thought and must make sense. It can be a question, a statement, or an exclamation!

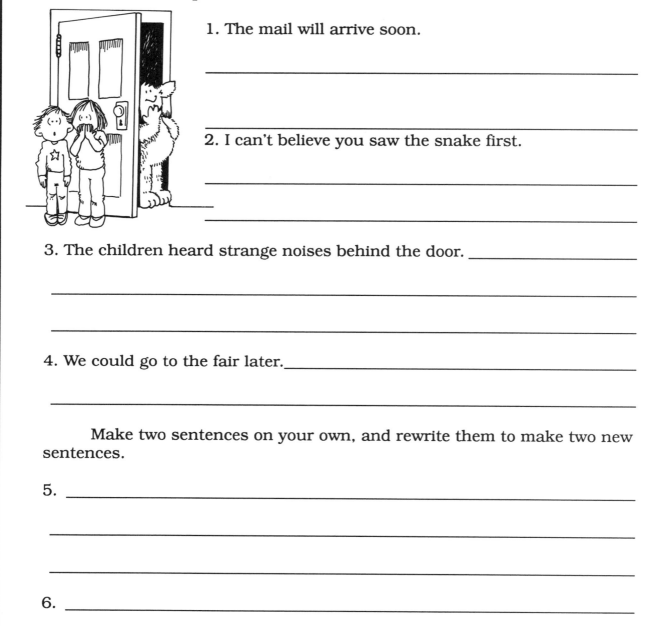

1. The mail will arrive soon.

_____

2. I can't believe you saw the snake first.

_____

_____

3. The children heard strange noises behind the door. _____

_____

_____

4. We could go to the fair later._____

_____

Make two sentences on your own, and rewrite them to make two new sentences.

5. _____

_____

_____

6. _____

_____

_____

Name _____

Rearranging, Modifying
© 1991 by Incentive Publications, Inc., Nashville, TN.

EYE CAN SEE!

Use your imagination or a real magnifying glass to look at these objects. On the lines beside each, tell what it could possibly become or be used for if it could grow to be:

1. as large as your hand
2. as large as your whole body
3. as large as a school bus

PAPER
CLIP
_____

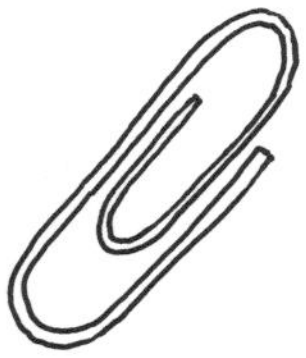

_____

_____

_____

_____ THUMBTACK

_____

_____ ERASER

_____

_____

_____ BUTTON

_____

_____

JACK _____

Name _____

Maximizing, Imagining
© 1991 by Incentive Publications, Inc., Nashville, TN.

P-P-PERPLEXED

PURPOSE
Imagining, conjecturing, transferring

PREPARATION
1. Each storystarter strip on the P-P-PERPLEXED activity page presents a nonhuman character caught in a perplexing situation. Add some of your own "starters" or ask students to contribute to the collection.

2. Cut the strips apart, and put each one in a separate envelope.

3. Print "P-P-Perplexed" on the cover of a notebook or folder designated to hold completed stories.

4. Place the envelopes, pencils, and writing paper with the notebook in a free-choice interest center. Add a study guide on which the following directions have been printed.

P-P-PERPLEXED!

1. Look up the word "perplexed" in the dictionary. Be sure you understand its meaning.

2. Choose one of the envelopes and read the storystarter inside.

3. Decide how and why the character might be perplexed.

4. Use the storystarter to write a first-person story. Imagine that you are the character/object, and create a story that tells how you feel.

5. Illustrate your story and add it to the P-P-PERPLEXED story book.

P-P-PERPLEXED

Activity Page

a bird with a broken wing

a just-wrecked automobile

a firefly in a bottle

a half-eaten ice cream cone

the last rose of summer

the only weed in a flower garden

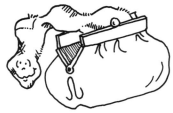

a dirty sock in a silk purse

a dolphin in a bathtub

a bar of soap in a waterfall

an ice cube on a hot tin roof

a raisin cookie in a baby's hand

a kitten trapped in a doghouse

Imagining, Conjecturing, Transferring
© 1991 by Incentive Publications, Inc., Nashville, TN.

CRITICAL CONNECTIONS

How carefully do you observe and think? Read each connected set of symbols to discover the sequence pattern. Fill in each blank space with the correct numeral, letter, or symbol.

1.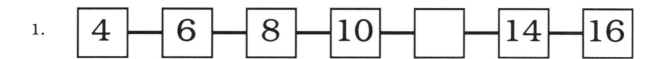

2.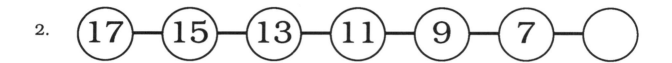

3.

4.

5.

6.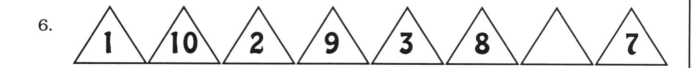

Name _____

Relating, Discovering, Projecting, Decoding
© 1991 by Incentive Publications, Inc., Nashville, TN.

THE WORD MACHINE

Feed each of the following through the Word Machine (your brain) and come up with a brand new, not-yet-heard-of word for each.

• a person who always puts his foot in his mouth

• a meal made of leftovers

• a machine that gives you a magic computer printout of all the answers to your math problems

• a homework assignment you hate

• an instrument that could measure whether or not a person is in love

• a day predicted by the weather report to be sunny, but turned out to be nasty

Name _____

Combining, Inventing
© 1991 by Incentive Publications, Inc., Nashville, TN.

MEET THE GIP

Hello! I'd like to introduce you to my friend the Gip. Let me describe him to you.

He has a heavy, stout body which is covered with coarse, bristly hair. His head and short, thick neck stick out in a straight line from his body. His body is horizontal to the ground. His head ends in a snout which looks like a fat pancake with large nostrils. He uses this snout to dig. He has tiny eyes and very sharp teeth. His short tail is curly. My friend has four feet with four toes on each foot.

(Look up any words you do not know in a dictionary. Then draw a picture of my friend the Gip in the space below.)

Keep your drawing a secret until you have finished. Then compare it with the drawings done by your classmates. Does the Gip's picture remind you of an animal you have met before?

Name _____

Interpreting, Visualizing
© 1991 by Incentive Publications, Inc., Nashville, TN.

IT'S REVERSIBLE!

PURPOSE

Reversing, brainstorming

PREPARATION

1. Propose to the class that this coming Friday will be a "Backward Day." Ask them to help you plan a day during which everything that would normally take place on this day would be done in reverse.

2. Brainstorm for suggestions, and write the ideas given on the chalkboard.

BACKWARD DAY!

- Wear clothes backward.

- Complete daily schedule from end to beginning.

- Walk backward.

- Spell names backward on name tags and call people by their "backward" names.

- Do all math problems backward. (If it says add, subtract; if it says multiply, divide.)

- Give directions in opposites, e.g., "Do not go to lunch" means "Go to lunch."

3. When the brainstorming session is complete, use the collected ideas to plan the day together.

4. Have a happy, crazy, backward Friday!

MIX 'N MATCH

Think of ways in which you could combine (put together) two or more objects on this page to create a brand new object. Find as many combinations as possible.

Using a different color for each set, draw lines to connect each set of objects you combine.

Describe or draw four of your new objects in the boxes below.

Name _____

Inventing, Combining
© 1991 by Incentive Publications, Inc., Nashville, TN.

ANY WAY YOU LOOK AT IT

Look carefully at figures A, B, C, and D. They are repeated in various ways in the nine boxes below. Shade in with your pencil each figure as you identify it. (It may appear backward, forward, sideways, or upside down.)

A   B   C   D

Name _____

Identifying, Differentiating, Comparing
© 1991 by Incentive Publications, Inc., Nashville, TN.

JUNGLE JOURNEY I

As you take your Jungle Journey, you will make several stops. Follow the instructions on each page.

Your first stop is PEBBLE BEACH.

Use the letters on the pebbles to make as many words with more than two letters as possible.

(You may use a pebble more than once in a word.)

Write your words in the sand.

Name _____

Composing, Assembling, Rearranging
© 1991 by Incentive Publications, Inc., Nashville, TN.

JUNGLE JOURNEY II

You are now in the VALLEY OF THE LITTLE PEOPLE.

Unscramble each set of letters to find the names of all the kinds of people who live here.

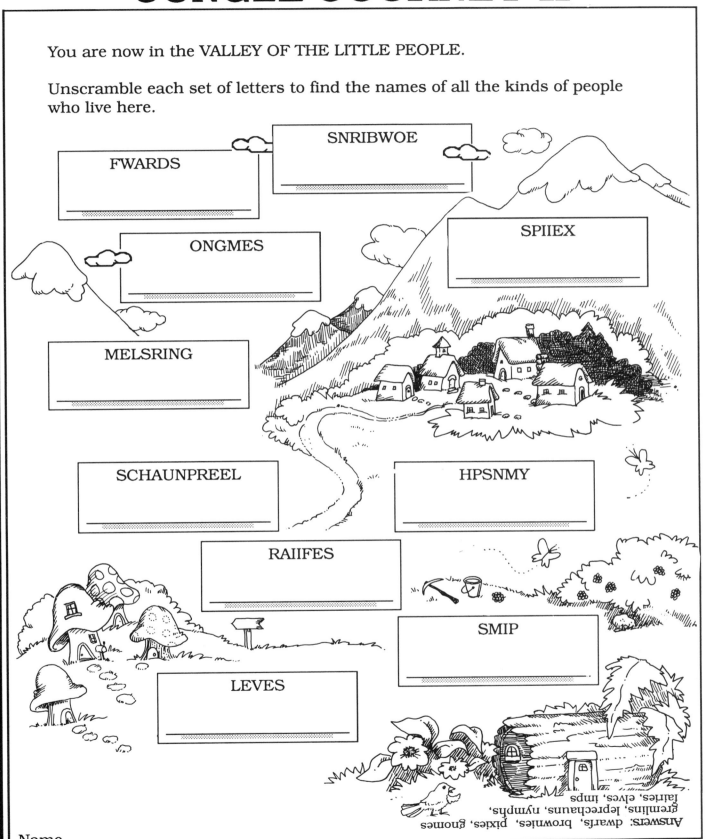

FWARDS
_____

SNRIBWOE
_____

ONGMES
_____

SPIIEX
_____

MELSRING
_____

SCHAUNPREEL
_____

HPSNMY
_____

RAIIFES
_____

SMIP
_____

LEVES
_____

Answers: dwarfs, brownies, pixies, gnomes gremlins, leprechauns, nymphs, fairies, elves, imps

Name _____

Rearranging
© 1991 by Incentive Publications, Inc., Nashville, TN.

JUNGLE JOURNEY III

This is CRITTER CROSSING.

Read the clues to write the names of the critters that come to this place.

1. + L + SOAP – S = _____

2. [bat] + C – B = _____

3. M + [house] – H = _____

4. [girl] + [ant] = _____

5. F + [box] – B = _____

6. [cat] + OR + [column] = _____

7. [pouring cup] + Q + [tree] = _____

Name _____

Reading, Translating, Interpreting
© 1991 by Incentive Publications, Inc., Nashville, TN.

FIELD OF FLOWERS

On each petal, write a word that goes with the word in the center of the flower.

Name _____

Associating, Combining
© 1991 by INCENTIVE PUBLICATIONS, Inc., Nashville, TN.

CREATURE FEATURE!

PURPOSE

Inventing, combining

PREPARATION

1. Reproduce the CREATURE FEATURES I and II work sheets.

2. Set aside a table or work area, and provide the following supplies: paste, scissors, felt-tip pens, crayons, pencils, stapler and staples, and stacks of the work sheets and the study guide.

3. Create a CREATURE FEATURE bulletin board where students can display their finished products.

PROCEDURE

CREATURE FEATURE STUDY GUIDE

You are about to create a creature never seen or heard of before! Let's see how inventive you are...

1. Before you begin, look carefully at the pages of shapes and think about what you want to make.

2. Cut out the shapes you will need.

3. Lay them on a clean sheet of paper and move them around until you get them just where you want them. Then paste them in place.

4. Draw lines or add squiggles and squirms to complete your creature.

5. Color your creature.

6. Add your new creation to the CREATURE FEATURE bulletin board your teacher has provided.

BONUS: Use your leftover shapes to create another invention that is NOT a living creature.

CREATURE FEATURE SHAPES I

Inventing, Combining
© 1991 by Incentive Publications, Inc., Nashville, TN.

CREATURE FEATURE SHAPES II

Inventing, Combining
© 1991 by Incentive Publications, Inc., Nashville, TN.

SPLIT DECISION

Do you ever have a hard time deciding the right thing to do? Pretend you must make a decision about each situation below.
1. Tell WHAT you would do.
2. Tell WHY.
3. Predict what MIGHT HAPPEN if you choose the wrong action.

When I go swimming, I aways take along...
a parakeet
a friend

Why?_____

_____

Prediction:_____

_____

When I cross the street, I always...
look both ways
run as fast as I can

Why?_____

_____

Prediction:_____

_____

_____

When I ride in a car, I always...
fasten my seatbelt,
hang out of the window

Why?_____

_____

If I give someone a knife or scissors, I always...
pitch it to him
hand it to her carefully

Why?_____

_____

Prediction:_____

_____

I always go down the stairs...
one at a time
two at a time

Why?_____

_____

Prediction:_____

_____

Name _____

Deciding, Conjecturing, Predicting
© 1991 by Incentive Publications, Inc., Nashville, TN.

HOW WOULD YOU FEEL? I

Write one complete sentence to tell the world how you would feel if you were:

in a barrel headed over Niagara Falls.

_____

_____ ☐

a turkey the day before Thanksgiving.

_____

_____ ☐

the last person on earth.

_____

_____ ☐

winner of $1 million prize.

_____

_____ ☐

the leader of your country at a very important dinner party.

_____

_____ ☐

caught stealing a cookie.

_____

_____ ☐

Name _____

Conjecturing, Summarizing
© 1991 by Incentive Publications, Inc., Nashville, TN.

HOW WOULD YOU FEEL? II

Write one complete sentence to tell the world how you would feel if you were:

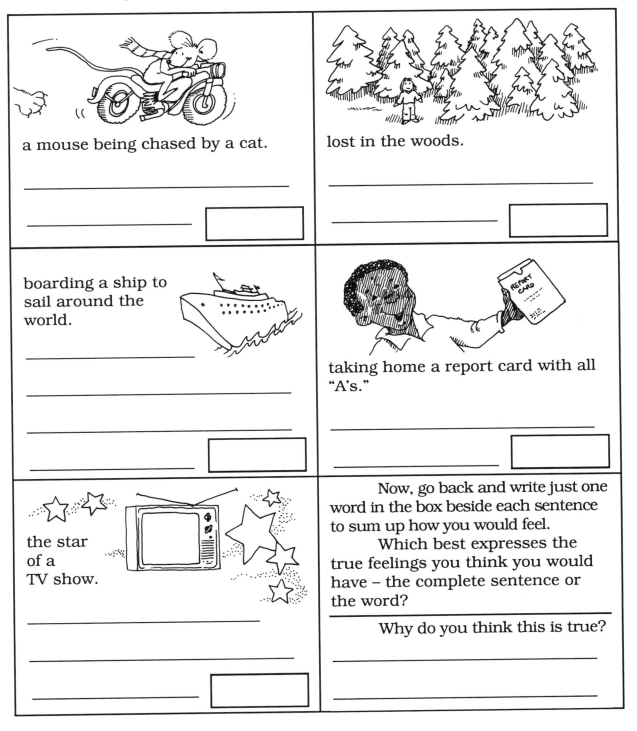

a mouse being chased by a cat.

_____

_____ [ ]

lost in the woods.

_____

_____ [ ]

boarding a ship to sail around the world.

_____

_____

_____ [ ]

taking home a report card with all "A's."

_____

_____ [ ]

the star of a TV show.

_____

_____

_____ [ ]

Now, go back and write just one word in the box beside each sentence to sum up how you would feel.

Which best expresses the true feelings you think you would have – the complete sentence or the word?

_____

Why do you think this is true?

_____

_____

Name _____

Conjecturing, Summarizing
© 1991 by Incentive Publications, Inc., Nashville, TN.

TWO SIDES OF ME

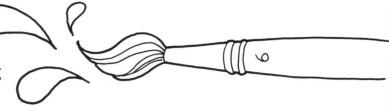

PURPOSE

Abstracting, creating, translating

PREPARATION

1. Provide tempera paints, colored chalk or a wide selection of crayons, and a large sheet (at least 18" x 24") of tagboard or heavy construction paper for each student.

PROCEDURE

1. Ask students to consider their personal qualities or attributes, both positive and negative.

2. Work together as a class to list as many of these as possible on the chalkboard.

3. Then ask each student to choose one positive quality and one negative quality which are especially characteristic of his/her own personality.

4. Direct students to select one or more colors that represent or express the essence of their positive qualities, and use these colors to create a design that suggests that quality. (This design should cover one side of the paper.)

Example: joyful, exuberant

5. Repeat the same process for the negative quality. (This design should fill the entire surface of the other side of the paper.)

6. Students may share their designs and ask classmates to guess the qualities illustrated.

FIVE FOREVER FRIENDS

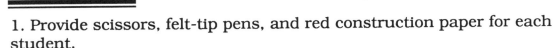

PURPOSE

Selecting, discussing, valuing

PREPARATION

1. Provide scissors, felt-tip pens, and red construction paper for each student.

2. Prepare a large heart shape for the bulletin board.

PROCEDURE

1. Direct each student to cut out a large heart shape from red construction paper.

2. Ask each student to think of the five words in the English language that he/she loves most and to write these on the heart. Beside each word, the student must write one reason why that word was chosen.

3. Divide the class into groups of four or five, and allow students to share their word choices and reasons.

4. After all words and reasons have been shared, direct the groups to carry on a discussion session during which they must choose only five of all the words presented as the most important of all.

5. Reassemble the class, and discuss the choices of each group. Following the discussion, ask students to vote for the eight to ten words they care most about. Write these on the heart prepared for the bulletin board, and display for the class to enjoy.